Teamwork

Story by Dawn McMillan
Illustrations by Pat Reynolds

D1275148

When Karina came to her new school, she had thought that making friends would be easy. At her other school, she had known everybody. Now, in this big school, she was lonely.

"Don't worry, Karina. You'll soon settle in," said Mom gently.

At first, Karina joined in all the games at school. When they played baseball, she hit the ball high into the air, past the fielders, and scored a home run almost every time. When they played basketball, she raced past the other children to score, again and again. And when they played tag, no one could catch her—not even Lisa, who had always been the best runner in the class.

Soon, the children stopped asking Karina to play.

"We've got enough players on our baseball team today," said Lisa.

Karina was surprised that they didn't want her on the team.

Every lunchtime, Karina stayed in the library.

Mr. Walker, her teacher, was worried about her. "Take a break, Karina," he said. "Go out with the other children. Have some fun!"

"It's all right, thanks, Mr. Walker," replied Karina. "I like to get my homework done early." She turned back to her books. "No one wants me on their team anyway," she thought.

One day, when Karina came home from school, she tossed her backpack down and started to cry.

"Karina!" said Mom in surprise. "What's wrong?"

Karina put her head in her hands. "I don't want to go to this school, Mom. I've tried to make friends. At lunchtime, the other kids don't ask me to join in their games. Everyone thinks that I'm a show-off!" she sobbed.

"Oh Karina! Of course you're not a show-off!" said Mom, as she put her arms around Karina. "It's not always easy to admit that someone is better than us at something that we enjoy. The other children probably feel a bit uncomfortable, that's all."

"But I don't try to be better than anyone else!" cried Karina. "It just happens that way."

"That's because you're good at sports," said Mom. "You always have been."

"But I want some friends," sobbed Karina. "What can I do?"

"Making friends at a new school can be difficult," said Mom. "Most of the children have known each other for a long time. Once they get to know you well, you'll make lots of friends."

The following week at school, Mr. Walker
put a poster on the class board:

FIELD HOCKEY
Hockey competition
in two weeks time
for Rooms 1-8.
Get a class team together!

The children gathered around.

Karina's heart jumped. Field hockey! She loved field hockey! "But I'm not going to tell anyone," she thought. "They wouldn't want me to play anyway."

"Let's make up a team!" said Lisa. "Who wants to play?"

Some of the children raised their hands excitedly.

"Who's good at hockey?" asked Tyler. "We'll need a coach."

Everyone was silent.

"Mr. Walker," called Lisa, "would you coach our team? Please!"

Mr. Walker laughed. "No teachers in this competition," he said. "You'll have to choose one of your classmates to be the coach."

Tyler and Lisa were disappointed. "No one in our class can play hockey very well," they muttered.

Karina took a deep breath. "I played hockey at my old school," she said quietly.

Lisa turned to her. "Really? Maybe you could coach us and play too," she said.

Karina grinned. "I'd love to!"

"Great!" said Tyler. "Thanks, Karina. Now, let's get our Room 3 team together!"

Soon there were eleven people who wanted to play.

The Room 3 team practiced every day. Karina taught them how to pass, stop, and dribble the ball. She also taught them how to flick the ball into the goal.

On the day of the competition, the team played really well. They won their first three games, and made it into the final game which was to be played during the afternoon.

Later that day, as they warmed up before the match, Lisa said, "I'm nervous. We're playing against Room 5—and they're **good**!"

"Yes," said Tyler. "They're going to be really hard to beat."

"But don't forget that we're a good team too!" said Karina. "Let's go!"

The teams ran out onto the field. The whistle blew, and the final match began. The players raced up and down the field. Then Karina dribbled the ball past a Room 5 defender, and flicked it into the goal. The crowd cheered!

"Good one, Karina!" called Lisa.

A few minutes later, Tyler ran down the field, dribbling the ball in front of him. When he was right in front of the goal, he flicked the ball to Lisa. She held her stick low and hit the ball into the goal. Now they were leading by two goals!

But Room 5 were determined to win, and they scored two goals early in the second half.

"Come on, Room 3!" shouted Karina. "We need another goal!"

The team raced up the field, flicking and passing the ball to each other.

"Keep going!" shouted Tyler. "We can do it!"

But the Room 5 players were too good. In the last minute of the game, they stole the ball and raced back up the field to score the winning goal.

15

After the game, Room 3 congratulated the other team. Then Lisa and Tyler went over to Karina.

"What a game!" puffed Tyler. "Thanks, Karina. We didn't win, but we wouldn't have gotten into the final game without you."

Karina laughed. "We were fantastic!"

Lisa laughed too. "Let's play again soon, Karina." Then she shouted across the field, "Watch out, Room 5! We're going to beat you next time!"